BUCKINGHA

A CENTURY IN PHO

Published jointly by
Buckinghamshire Federation of Women's Institutes
and Countryside Books

First published 1997
© Buckinghamshire Federation of Women's Institutes 1997

All rights reserved.
No reproduction permitted without the prior permission of the publisher:

COUNTRYSIDE BOOKS
3 Catherine Road
Newbury, Berkshire

ISBN 1 85306 454 8

FRONT COVER PHOTOGRAPH OF OXFORD STREET, HIGH WYCOMBE
IN THE EARLY 1900S
SUPPLIED BY RUBY SPENCER, LOOSELY ROW & LACEY GREEN WI

BACK COVER PHOTOGRAPH OF CORONATION STREET PARTY IN
HIGH WYCOMBE, 1953
SUPPLIED BY INEZ WRIGHT, HIGH WYCOMBE WI

Designed by Graham Whiteman

Produced through MRM Associates Ltd., Reading

Printed by J.W. Arrowsmith Ltd., Bristol

〜

CONTENTS

Walking along Bellfield Road, High Wycombe, in 1904 (Mrs M. Butler, Penn Street WI)

FOREWORD

As readers of this book will discover, Buckinghamshire's WI members have, once again, in conjunction with Countryside Books, come up trumps with a wealth of information, anecdotes and matters of interest arising from life in the County over the past one hundred years.

The photographs which follow will, I feel sure, fascinate and inform all who read this book.

As with the *Buckinghamshire Village Book* and *Buckinghamshire Within Living Memory*, new light has been cast on the County's past. Wherever the future may take us, this book will serve as a useful reminder of the twentieth century.

I do hope that you will enjoy browsing and reading this account of Buckinghamshire as seen through the eyes, and camera lenses, of our members.

Mrs Mary Miller
County Chairman

ACKNOWLEDGEMENTS

The photographs which appear in the following pages are but a few of the splendid collection provided by Buckinghamshire WI members, their families and friends.

It has been a privilege and a delight to have had a small part in the preparation of this book — a function greatly eased by the advice and information freely provided by people too numerous to mention individually.

I must, however, mention and thank in particular Margaret Ward, who has written the introductions to each chapter and edited the picture captions. Thanks also go to the staff at Countryside Books for their inspiration and endeavours in the production of another Buckinghamshire Federation publication.

If you enjoy reading this book as much as I have enjoyed its preparation, the Chairman's wishes will be fulfilled.

Mrs Sandra Connor
Project Co-ordinator

INTO THE 20TH CENTURY

(1900 – 1919)

Queen Victoria's death in 1901 marked the passing of a century and a way of life. The 'Old Queen' was widely mourned, but the Coronation of Edward VII the following year was celebrated in every town and village in Buckinghamshire.

Buckinghamshire was a very rural county at the turn of the century. Roads were still unmade and the horse reigned supreme in work and transport. Cars were few and far between, owned only by the wealthy, and people walked, bicycled or rode wherever they wanted to go. The horse-drawn carrier's cart was a lifeline for rural communities, bringing in goods and news from the outside world. The railways were essential for travel and communications further afield, and the growth of the railway works at Wolverton took men from the land into industry. Other industries were closely connected with the products of the land, like the thriving furniture makers and paper mills in High Wycombe.

However, the majority of men in Buckinghamshire worked on the big estates or on small farms and market gardens. The beauty of the countryside and its proximity to London had long attracted the wealthy, and 'the big house' employed many men and women in its locality, indoors and out. The squire and the rector were important figures of authority in most small communities.

Women had few avenues of employment open to them, though some made a living straw plaiting or lacemaking at home. Domestic service was often the only other option. The battle to gain female suffrage had a special interest for Buckinghamshire women, as Mrs Emmeline Pankhurst lived at Stewkley for a short time.

The better off in the early years of the century enjoyed the Edwardian summers and indulged themselves with the latest pleasures. The first indoor tennis court in the country was built at Loosley Row in 1900. It was the time of leisurely picnics, long and elegant dresses, and cricket on the village green. For the common folk, though, pleasures were few and simple. Holidays were very rare, and a day out at Burnham Beeches was often the highlight of the year for young and old alike.

Cottage homes were small and usually overcrowded, with open fires, oil lamps and candles, no indoor sanitation and water from the well or pump. Food was simple, home-grown and home-cooked. Many people lived in the area where their families had lived for generations.

Children attended all-age village schools, and rarely had the opportunity for education after the age of twelve. When they left school, they went straight to work. Throughout their working lives they feared illness or incapacity, and in old age the workhouse loomed. The first old age pensions were paid in 1909 and greeted with relieved gratitude. It was a hard world, but a peaceful and unpressured one, a time of great contrasts between rich and poor.

The century began with Britain at war in South Africa, and in 1914 Buckinghamshire men in their hundreds

Stone picking at Frieth c1906, a never ending job. Mr Barlow was the last man in Frieth to wear a smock; here it is tied round his waist. Sometimes he knapped flints for road surfacing, so his nickname was 'Knocker' Barlow. (Joan Barksfield – Frieth WI)

answered the call to fight the Hun. The years of the First World War were ones of suffering for the county's servicemen and their families, and food shortages at home encouraged the use of land girls on the farms. It was during these years that the first Women's Institutes were formed, as women left to cope alone supported and encouraged each other. Then, at last, the war ended and all over the county parties, fireworks and bonfires greeted the return to peace.

Below Frogmore Gardens,
High Wycombe in the
early 1900s.
(Ruby Spencer –
Loosley Row & Lacey
Green WI)

High Street, High Wycombe in the early 1900s. Bicycles and horse-drawn carts are the only traffic to contend with in a scene which looks familiar yet so very different from today.
(Ruby Spencer – Loosley Row & Lacey Green WI)

West Wycombe's main street, with chairs piled high on the pavement to the right. It is a very peaceful scene, despite being nearly midday.
(Ruby Spencer – Loosley Row & Lacey Green WI)

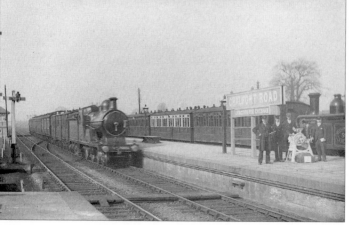

A train arriving at Chalfont Road station, Little Chalfont. The station is now known as Chalfont & Latimer.
(Elsie Geeves – Little Missenden WI)

*The windmill on Bledlow
Ridge c1918.
(Ruby Spencer –
Loosley Row & Lacey
Green WI)*

*Working on the railway near Seer Green – the line to
Beaconsfield and High Wycombe was opened c1906. The
arrival of the 'navvies' in a neighourhood was not the
cause for concern it had been in the more lawless days of
the railway fever of the 1800s.
(Mr W. Payne – c/o Seer Green WI)*

Feeding the cows in 1910 at Temple End, Hughenden Road, High Wycombe. This is now a public car park and the proposed site of a superstore. (Mrs M. Butler – Penn Street WI)

The Market Square, Old Amersham in 1900. Bicycles were popular for both men and women. The street itself would have been very muddy in winter, and dry and dusty in summer. (Jean Archer)

Amersham Broadway in 1905, with little danger for the children standing in the middle of the road!
(Jean Archer)

Left *'Rothschild cottages' in Winslow Road, Wingrave, 1905. They have a monogram 'H de R', and the date 1876, on a plaque denoting that they were built on land given to Hannah de Rothschild by her father on her marriage. The railings are still there today but the washing line has gone to make access to garages which today occupy most of the back gardens.*
(Mary Mountain – Wingrave WI)

Sunday morning at Frieth c1912. The young men of the village have their ferrets and terriers with them, set for a morning's sport. In the background is Colliers Farm rickyard, so they probably intended a ratting session.
(Joan Barksfield– Frieth WI)

13

Whaddon High Street. The buildings shown are the Reading Room, the Old Chapel just past the cottages, and the Haunch of Venison public house (the name a reminder of Whaddon Chase), now known as the Lowndes Arms. The tall postman is Alf Chandler, and this postcard was sent to him in 1904 when he was away in Hampshire with '1 Bletchley Coy, Camp 23 Field Army Brigade', with the reminder to 'bring this back with you'!
(Irene Smith – Winslow WI)

A rare view into a High Wycombe garden in the early years of the century. Older ladies were still to be seen in these very Victorian black dresses well into the 1920s and 1930s.
(Inez Wright – High Wycombe WI)

The Farnham Common Dairy delivery cart, with milk churn and measuring cup, c1918. For many years the milkman called with milk fresh from the dairy, ladled direct into the housewives' jugs.
(Judy Tipping – Templewood WI)

Making lace for the lace market at Bledlow Ridge. The income provided by lacemaking was often an essential element in housekeeping for labourers' families.
(Ruby Spencer – Loosley Row & Lacey Green WI)

Lacemakers in 1916 in an Olney garden. Lace was made and sold to a buyer, once a week, who provided the thread for the women. An average of twelve yards of lace were made by a woman in a week, working eight hours a day, five days a week, for which ten shillings were paid.
(Margaret Brimley – Olney WI)

A family visit to Mrs Cowley's cottage at The Cross, Nash in 1910. Her daughter Mary had come from London for the day, travelling from Euston to Bletchley station, and had borrowed the pram for baby Constance from Caroline, her sister. (Irene Smith – Winslow WI)

Workers and apprentices at a Wycombe cabinet factory. Once the main source of employment locally, today there are only a couple of furniture makers in the town. (Inez Wright – High Wycombe WI)

Above right *A load of chairs ready to be delivered, a common sight in the early 1900s at High Wycombe.* (Mrs M. Butler – Penn Street WI)

Right *Sweating on an iron cart tyre at Frieth c1910. The wooden wheel had been made at West & Collier's wood firm. The iron rim was made by the blacksmith, heated in the fire to expand it, and placed over the wooden wheel and quenched with water. The team are tapping the rim into place.* (Joan Barksfield – Frieth WI)

16

Levi Tearle and his son Mahlon, blacksmiths of Wing c1912. His sign says 'Cycles Repaired' as well as shoeing, and in the next decade smiths would also have to take on the challenge of the motor car.
(Mrs T. Shepherd – Wing WI)

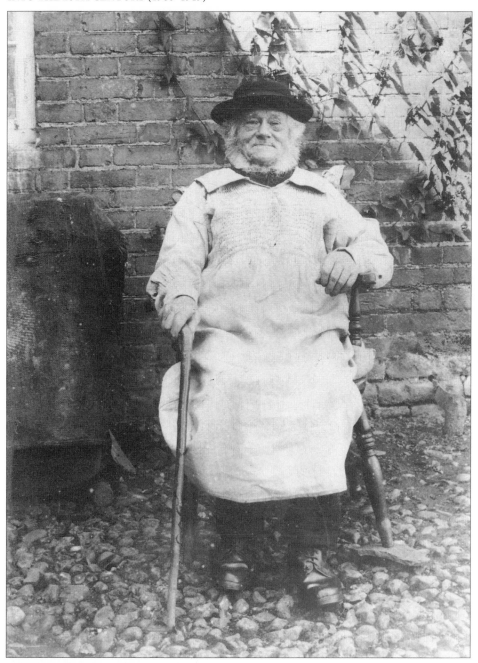

James Picton, who died in 1909 aged 91. He lived at
Peaceful Cottage, New Barn Lane, Seer Green, and is
wearing the typical farm labourer's smock. Some of his
descendants still live in the village.
(Mr W. Payne – c/o Seer Green WI)

Sheepshearing at Whitchurch in the 1900s, the shears driven by a hand-turned wheel.
(Maurice Foulger – c/o Whitchurch WI)

Below *Mr Bennett outside his stone-built farmhouse at Lower Weald, Calverton in the 1900s. Horse-drawn transport would still be more common than the motor car for some time. The lady looking through the window on the right seems to be dressed for going out as well – did the photographer know she was peeping at the scene outside?*
(Irene Smith – Winslow WI)

Henry Gross on the binder at Seer Green, c1910. He and his family lived at Butlers Cross, in the Bowles Farm cottages. Harvest and haytime brought everyone out to the fields – and carrying a gun meant rabbit for dinner.
(Mr W. Payne – c/o Seer Green WI)

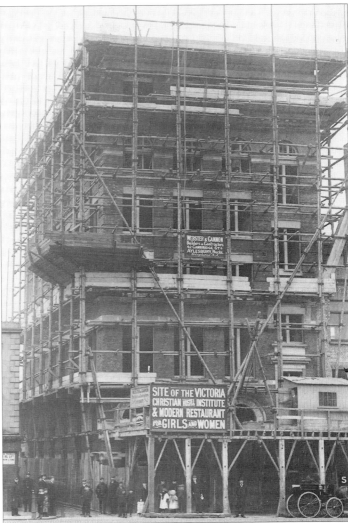

SITE OF THE VICTORIA
CHRISTIAN INSTITUTE
& MODERN RESTAURANT
FOR GIRLS AND WOMEN

The building firm of Webster & Cannon was founded at the end of the 19th century in Aylesbury and in its heyday had some 200 employees. It had its own brick pits (shown opposite) – now the site off Cambridge Street of MFI and other warehouses – and public buildings seemed to be their speciality, including Aylesbury Prison. When they worked elsewhere in the country (at Parkhurst Prison, for instance, or London banks) the labour force was taken from Aylesbury and lived on site in caravans.
(Shirley Rouse – Bledlow Ridge Morning WI)

Left The centre of Lane End in 1914. This is now the busy B482 road.
(Betty Twitchen – Lane End Evening WI)

THEN & NOW. Part of Marsworth village in 1906, and as it appears today. (Sylvia Frost – Marsworth WI)

The class of 1904–5 at Winslow Church of England school in Sheep Street. All the girls are wearing boots, and some have on the white pinafores which were so common amongst schoolchildren into the 1920s.
(Pam Allen – Winslow WI)

The Hon. Mrs Angela James, a great force for good in the local community all her life, started the pioneering Baby Welcome at Lane End in 1914, only the second such group in the country. The group still meets weekly in the village hall. (Betty Twitchen – Lane End WI)

A family group standing outside Bledlow Ridge school. Most villages had their own schools, all-age and with very few facilities. Labourers' children had little chance of staying on for further education and most left at about the age of 12. (Ruby Spencer – Loosley Row & Lacey Green WI)

Bottom *Off on the annual outing to Burnham Beeches by Wycombe Marsh Baptist church c1910.* (Inez Wright – High Wycombe WI)

Pupils and staff at Loudwater school at the turn of the century. (Inez Wright – High Wycombe WI)

Donkey rides were a popular attraction at Burnham Beeches. (Judy Tipping – Templewood WI)

Old Amersham High
Street, with the post office
staff celebrating the Relief
of Mafeking during the
South African War, May
1900.
(Jean Archer)

Seer Green football team
in 1900. Most villages
could support football and
cricket teams, and local
rivalries were fiercely
defended.
(Mr W. Payne – c/o
Seer Green WI)

Local army manoeuvres in
1907, 'Blue Force' entering
Winslow.
(Diana Kemp –
Winslow WI)

Right George Redrup of
Eden Cottages, Prestwood
– one of the many
Buckinghamshire men
who fought in the Great
War. He joined up in
November 1914 aged 15½
by declaring he was 19
years old. Wounded in
France, he was discovered
to be under age and was
discharged. As soon as he
was well he joined up
again in another regiment.
He was killed at the battle
of Aisne, on 15th June
1918, aged 19 years.
(Rose Redrup – Little
Chalfont Evening WI)

Helping to feed the nation
– vegetable gardening in
the First World War. Food
shortages hit poor people
especially hard.
(Inez Wright – High
Wycombe WI)

BETWEEN THE WARS

(1920 – 1938)

The 1920s brought an acceleration of the tendency for big country estates to break up, just one of the links with the past that were snapping after the war had ended. In 1929 West Wycombe village was sold by the Dashwood family to the Royal Society of Arts, to be passed on to the National Trust in 1934. Stowe estate was sold in 1921 in a great sale that lasted ten days, and in 1923 the house became the now famous public school.

Despite the Depression, mass production brought more affordable consumer goods onto the market. Cars became more common, bus services started up in rural areas and people became more mobile. The coming of the railway to the south of the county opened up commuting possibilities and enabled work to be sought further afield. Later, great sadness greeted the closure in 1935 of the Brill Tramway, one of the outposts of the Metropolitan Railway network.

The war was not forgotten and memorials were raised in every town and village. Over 5,000 people attended the unveiling of the Aylesbury war memorial. Armistice Day was marked each year by a heartfelt two minutes' silence.

Women got the vote after the war, though those under 30 had to wait until 1928! Many women found a political voice through the Women's Institute, which campaigned tirelessly on matters from health to housing in an effort to improve the lot of the country dweller. In 1933 the National Federation of Women's Institutes joined the Associated Country Women of the World, an organisation that is today represented at the UN.

The school leaving age went up to 14, but little else changed in schools. Children did, however, enjoy a freedom and security that later generations would not see.

Cherry blossom was one of the joys of springtime in the county, acres of cherry trees yielding a rich crop that was celebrated with Cherry Revels in many villages.

In 1929 Bekonscot Model Village opened, the oldest model village in the world and still attracting thousands every year. There were more opportunities for leisure activities, and the cinema became hugely popular. Pinewood Studios were built in 1934 at Iver Heath and the Rank Film Studios at Denham in 1936.

During the 1930s the fashionable group at the heart of the Cliveden Set became unfortunately associated with an attitude to Nazi Germany that was open to misunderstanding. As the decade wore on the threat of war became ever more ominous and soon it was clear that once again the men of Buckinghamshire would be called on to fight.

The Princess Royal opening the Girl Guides' Hall in Aylesbury in the 1920s.
(Elsie Geeves – Little Missenden WI)

1920 – 1938

Inside Wycombe
Marsh Paper Mill in
1936, sorting and
counting paper in 'the
Salle', the finishing
department. The
mill was the major
employer for both men
and girls from
Wycombe Marsh.
Today the mill is
derelict.
(Inez Wright – High
Wycombe WI)

31

*Woodlands Cottages,
Farnham Common c1920.
Just two-up, two-down
cottages, at one time there
were 30 children living in
eight of these ten homes.*
(Judy Tipping –
Templewood WI)

*A re-enactment in Olney
in 1926 of John Gilpin's
Ride (from local poet
William Cowper's poem*
The Diverting History of
John Gilpin*). As in the
poem the horse, on the left
in the photo, did actually
bolt! The Ride next took
place in 1931 and again in
1950, but was by then
proving difficult to stage
as the traffic had to be
stopped on the main road.*
(Margaret Brimley –
Olney WI)

Farnham Royal village in the 1920s with the old water pump in the centre, Dunkin's Bakery on the left and the Duke's Head public house on the right.
(Judy Tipping – Templewood WI)

Outside the post office at 'Meads', Wingrave in the 1920s. Thomas Jones built the house in 1895 and his wife Annie Woodward Jones was postmistress for 40 years, assisted by her daughter Polly (right) and granddaughter Sybil (left).
(Mary Mountain – Wingrave WI)

Off to do the shopping at Marlow from Hillarys Farm, Frieth in the early 1920s. Many families continued to rely on horse-drawn transport. (Mrs K. Hawes – Wheeler End WI)

The Hunt meet at the Crown, Little Missenden, c1920, an attraction to all ages.
(Doreen How – Little Missenden WI)

Ice breaking on the canal, approaching Cook's Wharf. As part of the Grand Union Canal, all heavy goods from London to Birmingham were trasnported along it, including coal. Today it sees mostly recreational use, though there are still one or two commercial boats. During cold spells the ice had to be broken to allow the boats through, by men 'rocking' the boat as the horses pulled it along the towpath.
(Sylvia Frost – Marsworth WI)

A funeral at Marsworth in February 1920 – Rebecca Seabrook and her daughter Ada Jane were drowned in the lock, and a canal barge was used as a hearse.
(Sylvia Frost – Marsworth WI)

An exciting Sunday outing by car around the lanes of Buckinghamshire in 1921, with all the family enjoying the open air.
(Mrs M. Butler – Penn Street WI)

The demands of motorised traffic were beginning to make themselves felt – this row of old houses in Old Amersham was demolished in the late 1920s for road widening.
(Elsie Geeves – Little Missenden WI)

A works outing by charabanc in 1928. Moving at about 12 mph, this was a stately way to travel. The collapsible hood at the back could be pulled right over if it rained.
(Elsie Geeves – Little Missenden WI)

Left Men who had swapped the mud of the trenches for that on a building site in 1920. 'At least one of these men was a Marsh man, and as no one in Wycombe Marsh had a car at that time, the site was within walking or cycling distance.' (Inez Wright – High Wycombe WI)

Workers waiting to be paid at Thomas Glenister's factory in Hughenden Road, High Wycombe in the 1920s – wages were handed out through the office window. Daniel Glenister began the firm in 1839.
(Mrs M. Butler – Penn Street WI)

Left *Whaddon Guides and Brownies in 1927, the year they were formed. The photo was taken at the rear of the post office in the High Street.*
(Irene Smith – Winslow WI)

Missenden Abbey at Great Missenden c1920 – then a private residence, and today an adult education centre.
(Elsie Geeves – Little Missenden WI)

Bottom right *Wycombe Marsh Bridge and Paper Mill, c1925. 'I remember as a child leaning over the wall of the bridge on our way to school to see the colour of paper being made that day. The river might be bright red, blue or green. Later, this pollution was controlled.'*
(Inez Wright – High Wycombe WI)

39

Haymakers taking a break at Whitchurch in the 1920s.
(Maurice Foulger – c/o Whitchurch WI)

Threshing corn at Alderman's Farm, Whitchurch in the early 1930s, the power provided by a steam engine.
(Maurice Foulger – c/o Whitchurch WI))

The wedding of Eva Smith to Sidney Ward in 1924 at Whaddon. The peace of this setting, in a gamekeeper's cottage garden, is today shattered by heavy traffic along a Milton Keynes grid road. (Irene Smith – Winslow WI)

Harvesting is thirsty work and as Mr Leaver senior (here with his son) was also landlord of the Yew Tree Inn at Frieth in the 1920s the stone jar probably contained beer. However, many harvesters preferred to drink cold tea with their 'bit' at midday and wait to savour a pint at the pub in the cool of the evening. (Joan Barksfield – Frieth WI)

41

The bakery – Chowles & Sons – in Horn Street, Winslow c1937. With one huge bread oven, coal-fired, they made bread, cakes, pastries and pies to be sold in Winslow and by van in the villages around. The enterprise was sold to Becketts in the 1950s and baking finally ended in 1990. To the left of the bakery, William Chowles (junior) had a watchmaking and jewellery business; he invented an altimeter which was commissioned by aviator Amy Johnson on one of her frequent visits to Winslow.
(Pam Allen – Winslow WI)

High Street, Seer Green in the 1930s, with the Jolly Cricketers in the right foreground. Cars were taking the place of bicycles and horse-drawn waggons in day to day life.
(Mr W. Payne – c/o Seer Green WI)

Whitchurch High Street in the 1930s. The smell of the hot tar was believed to be good for all kinds of ailments.
(Maurice Foulger – c/o Whitchurch WI)

A peaceful view of Bisham church, Marlow in the early 1930s.
(Mrs J. Hamilton – Taplow & Hitcham WI)

Mursley Cricket Club, winners of the Bucks District League in 1937. (Irene Smith –Winslow WI)

In many villages water was still fetched from the well or pump every day. During the drought in 1933 this group of villagers was waiting at Quainton for Jo Mole to unlock the pump at 6 pm.
(Jean Ridgway – Quainton WI)

Folk dancing in Aylesbury Road, Wendover to celebrate the Jubilee of George V in 1935. Mr Newton played the violin and his wife played piano, perched on a horse-drawn cart. Two years later there were again celebrations across the county when George VI was crowned. (Miss B. Newton – Wendover Evening WI)

Wing Congregational chapel Sunday school anniversary tea on a local farm in 1936.
(Mrs T. Shepherd – Wing WI)

Opening day of the children's playground at the side of the Three Horseshoes, Seer Green in the 1930s. A see-saw, swings and a slide were exciting new games for the local children.
(Mr W. Payne – c/o Seer Green WI)

47

THE SECOND WORLD WAR

(1939 – 1945)

On 3rd September 1939 the Prime Minister, Neville Chamberlain, informed the nation that we were once more at war with Germany. After the nerve-wracking sound of the first air raid sirens, an uneasy peace descended and we entered the period of the 'phoney war', before Dunkirk woke us all to the threat of invasion.

Civilians were more involved in this war than they had ever been before. Windows had to be blacked out at night, and panes of glass criss-crossed with tape to prevent damage from blast. Signposts were removed to foil enemy parachutists, station nameplates taken down, and iron railings disappeared for the war effort, or so they told us. Sandbags protected important buildings and air raid shelters were dug or built – homes were issued with Anderson shelters for the garden, or Morrison shelters for inside. Gas masks were issued and had to be carried at all times.

Rationing was imposed from the start and it was later said that the British diet was the most healthy it had ever been – before or since. Queues formed wherever extra food or other goods could be found – and some people joined any queue on principle! Women's Institutes opened village Jam Centres, with government backing, so as to preserve the fruit and vegetable harvest. Queen Elizabeth visited Institutes in Buckinghamshire to see the scheme in action.

Boy Scouts covered up the Whiteleaf Cross on the Chilterns above Princes Risborough, which was thought to be a marker for enemy planes to find Chequers. Buckinghamshire suffered its share of air raids and bombs, though none to compare with those that reduced so much of London to rubble. At night the fires in London could be seen reflected in the sky, and searchlights streaked the sky.

Strangers of all sorts came to the County. Children were evacuated from London and billeted in villages and towns, disrupting schooling for both themselves and local children. Industries and businesses were also evacuated from the city, and many of those that came to High Wycombe, never went back. The quiet country town that High Wycombe had been for so long was gone for ever.

German and Italian prisoners of war could be seen working in the fields, alongside the land girls who kept food production high at a time when every harvest was vitally important. Bomber Command also came to Buckinghamshire, and Winston Churchill gave a speech in 1942 from the same balcony porch in High Street, High Wycombe that Disraeli had used when he was electioneering in 1832. The Abbey at Aston Abbotts was home for a while to the Czech government-in-exile.

The Canadian Red Cross Hospital opened at Taplow, and Stoke Mandeville Hospital took in badly wounded servicemen as well as the overflow of civilian casualties from the Middlesex Hospital. At Hyde House, badly burned servicemen recuperated after Sir Archibald MacIndoe's pioneering plastic surgery.

1939 – 1945

George VI at
Wycombe Abbey
School c1942,
when the school
had been
requisitioned by
the Army.
(Mrs S. Moore –
Seer Green &
Jordans WI)

Over 12,000 people, including the country's most eminent mathematicians and academics, were employed at the Bletchley Park secret government code and cipher school. Their development of the Enigma code-breaking machine was said by Churchill to have shortened the war by three years.

Airfields sprang up, used by both the RAF and the American Air Force, and as D-Day approached it was apparent that American soldiers were massing in preparation. On the day itself, the sky was full of planes and gliders on their way to the beaches of Normandy.

VE Day in May 1945 was an occasion day of great celebration, with numerous bonfires, and hoarded food was brought out for street parties so that the children everywhere could have a wonderful day to remember.

The sandbagged Chief Warden's post for the Wycombe District was formerly the office of builder's merchant E.J. West (Penn) Ltd. It was also an ARP siren post. It was manned 24 hours a day and air raid warnings were in force almost every night. As enemy bombers passed overhead they occasionally jettisoned their load and bombs fell near Hazelmere and in Penn Woods; a landmine fell in Great Kimble village. Fortunately there were no serious injuries or damage.
(Madeleine Morris – Downley Evening WI)

Drayton Parslow's Civil Defence fire-fighting team in 1940.
(Elsie Willis – Drayton Parslow WI)

Right The wartime Auxiliary Fire Service in High Wycombe. 'When my father was a part time fireman, if there was a call-out during the day the fire siren would go, but during the night a bell would ring in the kitchen (no phones then) and out he would go, pedalling furiously away on his bicycle to the station.' Some of the local men were based down in Southampton for a while, helping to deal with the effects of the heavy bombing on the south coast ports.
(Madeleine Morris – Downley Evening WI)

The local Air Raid Precaution (ARP) unit after a demonstration on The Rye, High Wycombe. This exercise probably dates from about 1938–9, when preparations for war were well under way, though the reality of it still came as a shock on 3rd September 1939.
(Madeleine Morris – Downley Evening WI)

The local Air Training Corps (ATC) and Girls Training
Corps (GTC) in Quoiting Square, Marlow. They met up
prior to marching through Marlow to a church parade at
All Saints' church, after which they were on parade in the
Causeway to be inspected by Brigadier Wilkinson.
(Diana Simpson – Marlow Common WI)

Right and below In 1940 hospital supplies were delivered in bulk to Hall Barn, Beaconsfield and then sorted and parcelled by Red Cross volunteers for delivery (by horse and cart) to various hospitals. (The Dowager Lady Burnham)

An open air service held in the cherry orchard behind the Three Horsehoes pub at Seer Green in the 1940s. Mr Sid Bateman is playing the organ; the Baptist lay preacher Mr Fred Saunders is to the right holding his hat; and the Vicar of Holy Trinity is standing on the trestle table.
(Mr W. Payne – c/o Seer Green WI)

Much of the county remained untouched by war – blacksmith Tom Woodruff at Wingrave in 1940. The forge itself is now a garage. The sign belonged to George Rickard, a blind mat maker who lodged at the forge.
(Mary Mountain – Wingrave WI)

High Street, Amersham in 1940, when sheep were still herded along the main road.
(Jean Archer)

Queen Elizabeth's visit to Hyde Heath in 1940, where she met WI members preparing fruit for canning. The Bucks Examiner *described the occasion: 'Few people knew of her visit until an hour or two before she arrived, but the news quickly spread through the village and there was quite a crowd assembled in the road to see her arrive and to cheer her when she left.' Lady Denman, Bucks WI President, is in the background.*
(Irma Dolphin – Hyde Heath WI)

No 268 Prisoner of War Camp at Norduck Farm, Aston Abbotts. The site was first occupied by part of the Czech government-in-exile, housed in Nissen huts. The Nissen huts needed renovation subsequently, and meanwhile the tented camp seen in the photograph, 1945–6, was in use by German prisoners.
(Mary Mountain – Wingrave WI)

Bletchley Park (1) was taken over by government code-breaking staff in 1939. The secret work carried out there has subsequently become famous. By 1943 the world's first electronic programmable computer was operational (2), greatly assisting in the work of breaking enemy military codes. In these buildings (3) German, Italian and Japanese ciphers were broken, helping to shorten the war and save many lives.
(Ann Turl – courtesy Bletchley Park Trust Ltd)

1

2

At the Buckinghamshire 'War Ag' depot, Amersham.
Land girls lived locally and were allocated to farmers in
the area. Their work was essential to keep Britain's food
production going during these days of shortages and
hardship.
(Mrs P. Cox – Ballinger Evening WI)

3

Below The VE Day
children's party, Keep Hill
Drive, High Wycombe.
(Madeleine Morris –
Downley Evening WI)

Far left Peter Lloyd, an Observer with 40 Squadron RAF, was one of Buckinghamshire's men overseas. In 1942 he baled out over the desert in Egypt and spent the rest of the war in a German prisoner of war camp; afterwards he came back to live in the Marlow area.
(Diana Simpson – Marlow Common WI)

The Lane End Girls' Friendly Society entry for the peace celebrations on 8th June 1946 – they were 'GI Brides' going to the US on the Queen Mary.
(Betty Twitchen – Lane End Evening WI)

Carnival floats on the recreation ground at Wingrave, as part of the VE Day celebrations.
(Mary Mountain – Wingrave WI)

Above After the war the men who had served and died were remembered in every town and village. This was the ceremony of dedication of the war memorial tablets to the men from Lane End who died during the war.
(Betty Twitchen – Lane End Evening WI)

THE POST-WAR YEARS

(1946 – 1959)

The freezing winter of 1947 seemed to epitomise post-war Britain, where so much was still rationed and so many were still homeless after the destruction of the wartime bombing. Even bread did not come off ration until 1948. But there was new hope in the air too, as the Welfare State was created and the promise made that every citizen would be supported, when necessary, from the cradle to the grave. The National Health Service brought medical attention to all, without the doctor's bill!

Industry was moving out of London after the war, and London's loss was Buckinghamshire's gain as Wolverton and Bletchley grew.

Getting back to normal was on everyone's minds and old customs were remembered. In 1948 Olney's annual Shrove Tuesday Pancake Race was revived. Its fame even spread abroad, and firm and lasting links were forged with the town of Liberal in Kansas, USA in 1950. In 1954 a pageant and other events celebrated the 400th anniversary of Buckingham's municipal charter.

On the land, mechanisation was fast replacing the working horse and also leading to a considerable loss of jobs. Soon the combine harvester would take over the harvest, ending an ancient tradition that had once seen all the family out in the fields.

Car ownership was growing fast, and roads had to be improved; the first motorway, the M1, was opened in 1959. Already concerns were being voiced about the effects of traffic on towns and villages ill equipped to cope with it.

Changes in land ownership continued. The Astor family had given Cliveden House to the National Trust with an endowment in 1942, and in 1954 the 3rd Viscount gave the Trust Taplow Court Woods as well. Three years later, the art collection of James de Rothschild was sold, and Waddesdon Manor was bequeathed to the National Trust.

The 1951 Festival of Britain opened the decade with a flourish, and the conquest of Everest and the Coronation of the young Queen Elizabeth II in 1953 were great boosts to national morale. A new Elizabethan Age was dawning. The Coronation, televised live for the very first time, also gave an added impetus to TV ownership, and by 1959 nearly two-thirds of all households would have a set. Fridges, washing machines and Hoovers were also popular, and were no longer the preserve of the wealthy. A new emphasis on youth developed and 'teenagers' emerged – much to the bafflement of their elders.

Deep snow in Well Street, Buckingham, March 1947. That winter was particularly hard, and made worse by the continuing rationing of food and coal. (Miss H. Walker – Buckingham WI)

1946 – 1959

Florence Callow kissing the verger after winning the Olney Pancake Race in 1950. (Florence Mynard – Olney WI)

At Taplow Horse Show in the early 1950s, The Show was started in 1945 by Mrs Eileen Law, and celebrated its 50th anniversary in 1995. Princess Anne made one of her first competitive appearances here, supported by the Queen. It is now recognised as the first of the major shows. (Taplow & Hitcham WI)

Left *The Lane End Methodist Guild Tea in January 1947, a function that began before the First World War and continued every year up to the 1970s. The members of the Guild used to go carol singing round the village, carrying their little harmonium, to raise money for this event, which was greatly looked forward to locally.*
(Betty Twitchen – Lane End Evening WI)

'My father E.W. Currie with his new Triumph Mayflower, 1948.' More and more families were finding the car an essential part of their lives.
(Mrs J. Porter – Stoke Poges WI)

The turning to Little Missenden in the mid 1950s, before the dual carriageway was built.
(Doreen How – Little Missenden WI)

THEN & NOW. The Olney Pancake Race in 1950 and today. The race dates back to the 15th century, but in February 1950 it achieved international dimensions. After the war the ladies of Liberal in Kansas, USA had begun their own Pancake Race, inspired by Olney, and in 1950 they challenged their English counterparts to a race for the Transatlantic Pancake Trophy for the first time. The winner that year was Florence Callow of Olney, who remembers: 'I was 18 years old when I won the race, and that was the first time America had challenged us, so it was quite a big day for us in Olney. I beat America by about seven seconds.' (Florence Mynard – Olney WI; Anne Larr – Willen WI)

Members of the St John Ambulance Brigade in 1950 at Bletchley. (Ann Turl – Stony Stratford WI)

The Girl Guides Banner Service parade at Aylesbury in 1951, led by Lady Burnham, Bucks County Commissioner. Notice the signs on the building behind referring to the Civil Defence Office – the Cold War meant that we were still in a state of readiness should the worst happen. (The Dowager Lady Burnham)

Mrs Emilie Life, retiring head teacher of Chenies primary school, in July 1951 with some of the pupils who were helping to build her new house – 168 of the children laid bricks inscribed with their name. Elaine Griffiths, aged five, is shown laying her brick. (Mrs M. Griffiths – Chorleywood WI)

Tobogganing down from Rectory Wood to Old Amersham in 1950. (Jean Archer)

*Gathered for the
Coronation party at
Pinewood Drive, Bletchley.*
(Ann Turl – Stony
Stratford WI)

*Market Square,
Buckingham decorated for
the Coronation.*
(Miss H. Walker –
Buckingham WI)

*At Frieth in 1953 the
parish councillors planted
a flowering cherry tree on
the green to commemorate
the Coronation. The curate
blessed it and the staff and
children of Frieth school
sang* All Things Bright
and Beautiful. *The tree is
still flowering well.*
(Joan Barksfield –
Frieth WI)

THE SIXTIES AND SEVENTIES

(1960 – 1979)

The Swinging Sixties brought in a new age of fashion, music and attitudes. With the arrival of mini skirts and the Beatles, things would never be the same again. The age of majority was reduced to 18 in 1968. Anything seemed possible as man walked on the moon in 1969. Unfortunately, the Seventies also brought us industrial conflict and the three-day week.

High Wycombe was one of the boom towns of the South East in the 1960s, and its wide diversity of industries helped it to ride out the coming recession. Milton Keynes, Britain's newest city, was born; in 1967 the population was 40,000, by 1988 it had risen to 137,000.

Traffic continued to increase as roads took haulage away from the railways. During the early 1960s, the Beeching Axe fell on many branch lines, including North Aylesbury.

The farthing went out of circulation in 1960, and in 1971 decimal currency replaced pounds, shillings and pence. Two years later, Britain joined the EEC. The 1960s had seen a consumer boom and new shopping centres were built – the Octagon in High Wycombe and Friars Square in Aylesbury. Sixties architecture would not always stand the test of time – in 1966 Aylesbury's new County Hall was known as Pooley's Folly after its architect. Tall buildings, office blocks and ring roads blighted towns and left a lasting legacy.

In 1963 the Profumo scandal nearly brought down the government, involving Cliveden House, call girls, English politicians and a Russian diplomat! A year earlier Buckinghamshire had been in the news when the Great Train Robbery took place near Cheddington, with the robbers' hideout located at Leatherslade Farm, near Oakley.

Further education was now open to all, young and old. In 1970 the Open University began, based at Walton Hall in south Milton Keynes. Three years later the University College was founded at Buckingham, independent of government funding, and took its first students in 1976.

Local government reorganisation carved off bits of the old county of Buckinghamshire in 1974, and the busy industrial town of Slough found itself in Berkshire.

A celebrity horse – Sefton – retired to the Rest Home for Horses at Speen after the Knightsbridge bomb attack on the Household Cavalry. In 1977 a different kind of celebrity, Sir John Betjeman, was at Stoke Poges, following the repair of the Gray Memorial outside the church. That same year the Rothschilds' Mentmore Towers was sold, eventually being taken over by the Transcendental Meditation Movement. Five years earlier the Duke and Duchess of Kent had sold their home Coppins at Iver.

The threat that acres of Buckinghamshire countryside would disappear under the runways of London's proposed third airport brought communities out to fight. Stewkley, Wing and Cublington enlisted huge support in their successful campaign of 1973.

1960 – 1979

Queen Elizabeth
The Queen
Mother paid a
visit to Stowe and
the Royal Latin
School,
Buckingham on
10th June 1963.
(Miss H. Walker
– Buckingham
WI)

Farnham Common in the early 1960s.
(Judy Tipping – Templewood WI)

The Bull Ring, Buckingham in 1965, a peaceful scene.
(Miss H. Walker – Buckingham WI)

Top right *The widening of the bridge on Hatters Lane, High Wycombe c1964. As roads became busier, roadworks began to loom large in our lives!*
(Janet Allum – High Wycombe Morning WI)

Replacing Little Chalfont railway bridge prior to widening the road. The bridge was put into place during one weekend in early spring 1975. (Pat Warburton – Amersham Old Town WI)

Gerry Davies of Hambleden in 1970 (1) and Bert Haywood at Wingrave in 1973 (2). Although the old craft of hedge layering was common practice in the first half of this century, it went into decline as hedges were grubbed up to make larger fields and electric fencing was used for stock, so this was a welcome sight in the 1970s. Layering is a skilled job; stakes are hammered in at intervals, and the growing saplings nicked at the base to enable them to bend without splitting, before being woven between the stakes. (Joan Barksfield – Frieth WI; Mary Mountain – Wingrave WI)

2

Above 'Farmers Talk' – market day in 1963 at Bletchley, behind Duncombe Street. The gentleman on the left is not known, but the others were (l. to r.) Mr Hector Ramsay of Windmill Hill Farm, Mr John Wright of Bletchley Leys Farm, and Mr Bill Gregory of Park Hill Farm, Whaddon. (Mr D. Daniels c/o Irene Smith – Winslow WI)

The Buckinghamshire Federation of Women's Institutes' Golden Jubilee was held at Stowe in 1970. (Miss H. Walker – Buckingham WI)

Signing the Charter twinning Buckingham with Joinville in France, 2nd September 1968. (Miss H. Walker – Buckingham WI)

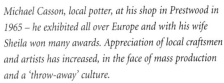

Michael Casson, local potter, at his shop in Prestwood in
1965 – he exhibited all over Europe and with his wife
Sheila won many awards. Appreciation of local craftsmen
and artists has increased, in the face of mass production
and a 'throw-away' culture.
(Val Corteen – Prestwood Evening WI)

A charity stall at the High Wycombe Show in 1960. The Show was started in 1947 with the intention of appealing to all ages – there were horse-jumping events, agricultural classes, competitions for home-made foods and wines and for home produce. 'My father became a life member at the start and each year received two tickets by post. It was the one day of the year he had to himself. He set off early with his packed lunch and didn't come home till late.' The Show still takes place, though it is no longer so central to local life.
(Inez Wright – High Wycombe WI)

*In 1967, Milton Keynes, Britain's newest city, was born in
the north of the county. Over 20,000 acres of countryside
were taken over, encompassing the existing towns of
Bletchley, Stony Stratford, Wolverton, and New Bradwell,
plus 13 villages and the brick fields south west of Bletchley.*
(Milton Keynes Development Corporation)

Long Crendon festival in
1970. It had been
suggested by the late John
Butler as an event to
'bring to our village life a
week's enjoyment to suit
all ages and tastes.' The
procession of floats
through the village was
just one of the
components. It was held
annually until the early
1970s.
(Joan Pace – Long
Crendon WI)

Below The parade starts
off at Nash, part of the
celebrations for the
Queen's Silver Jubilee in
1977.
(Mary Bowden – Nash
WI)

MODERN TIMES

~

(After 1980)

As Buckinghamshire approaches the 21st century, it is a county of great contrasts – between the busy and growing centres like Milton Keynes, Aylesbury, High Wycombe and Buckingham, and the tranquil villages that dot the countryside. New 'high-tech' industries have found homes in the towns, while old crafts like straw plaiting and lace-making have found new devotees in town and village alike.

Conservation of the countryside, and of the best of the past, has become ever more important. The renewal of activity on the Grand Union Canal is just one aspect of the ways in which the past is being integrated into modern life.

The Great Storm that swept across southern England in the autumn of 1987 caused dreadful damage to the woodlands in just one night – in Burnham Beeches one casualty was 'His Majesty', a 600 year old tree. In another calamity, Missenden Abbey was destroyed by arson, but has now been rebuilt as an adult education centre.

In 1987 a new rail station opened, Haddenham and Thame Parkway. Commuting has become very important to the County's inhabitants, particularly in the south. Farming has changed almost beyond recognition over the century and today many farmworkers' cottages have been bought by people who commute to work in the towns and cities, which has had its own effects on village life. So many village shops and businesses have gone, though greater awareness of the threat has led to increased support from customers. The rise of supermarket shopping, and then of the out-of-town hypermarkets in the 1980s, hit small shops hard. In 1980 Margaret Thatcher opened Milton Keynes' new shopping centre, and many of the 1960s centres in other towns were redeveloped in the era of the shopping mall.

One of the greatest problems the County faces, in common with the rest of England, is the huge growth in car ownership and traffic congestion. With the opening of the M25, Buckinghamshire had four motorways within its boundaries, with all that implies for noise, congestion and pollution. In 1987 the Amersham bypass was completed, relieving at least this high street from heavy traffic, but a long term solution is no nearer.

During the 1990s the commemoration of the 50th anniversaries of the events of the Second World War brought communities together in street parties all over the County.

Computers, mobile phones, the Internet, television – all have revolutionised the way we work and play in the last decade of the 20th century.

Inside Markham's ironmonger's shop in Buckingham, which closed in January 1986. It was an old family business, started over a century before. (Miss H. Walker – Buckingham WI)

After 1980

Schoolchildren
dancing round the
maypole in
Buckingham town
centre, May Day
1980.
(Pat Carter –
Westbury &
Shalstone WI)

The demise of the traditional red telephone box, 1989.
(Inez Wright – High Wycombe WI)

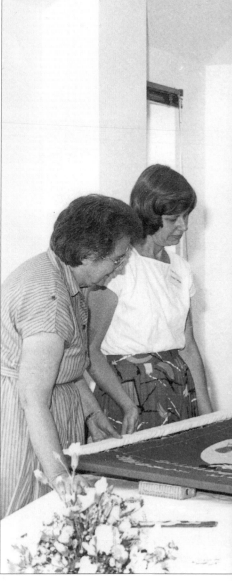

Princess Diana outside Wycombe Guildhall after opening the Reggie Goves Centre in September 1989, and meeting members of High Wycombe Morning WI.
(Inez Wright & Joyce James – High Wycombe WI)

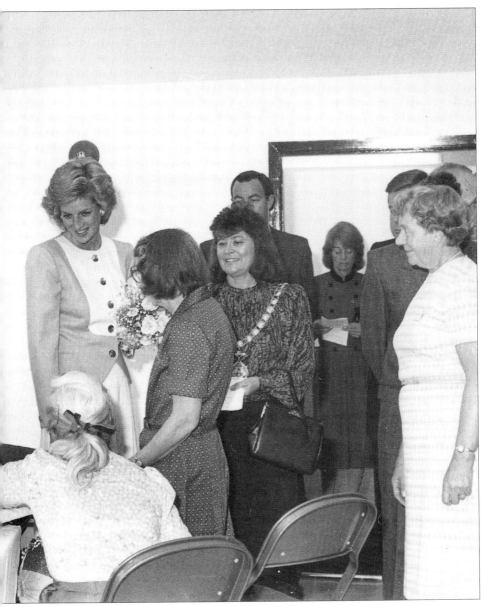

THEN & NOW. The windmill at Lacey Green – derelict in 1968 and restored in 1996. (Doris Oliver – Loosley Row & Lacey Green WI)

Right *One hundred year old Mrs Florence Marshall being presented to the Queen on 13th March 1992, in Milton Keynes to open the new City Church.* (Miss A. Lloyd – Stony Stratford WI)

MODERN TIMES (AFTER 1980)

*THEN & NOW. From the Ship Bridge, Marsworth, looking towards Cheddington, today and in 1920, and (**right**) Mr and Mrs Chamberlain of the Ship Inn in 1900.*
(Sylvia Frost – Marsworth WI)

Marriotts' bicycle shop
another family concern,
that opened in
Buckingham c.1920. It
closed in January 1986.
(Miss H. Walker –
Buckingham WI)

*Drayton Parslow
schoolchildren maypole
dancing outside the Three
Horseshoes on May Day 1989.*
(Elsie Willis – Drayton
Parslow WI)

Part of the May Feast Procession at Whitchurch 1991.
(June Nicol – Whitchurch WI)

THEN & NOW.
Cuddington post office at
the turn of the century and
today, now a private house.
Annie Jackman, standing
nearest the horse in the
early photo, was the
postmistress until she
married at the age of 30.
She made local deliveries
by horse and cart.
(Madeleine Morris –
Downley Evening WI)